GET FIRED UP!
ABOUT YOUR LIFE

BECAUSE IF YOU DON'T
WHO WILL?

ERNEST 'DAVE' BENNERMAN

ISBN: 978-1522700050
ISBN: 1522700056

Acknowledgments

I would like to dedicate this book to those who have been a castaway in life; so many people told you that you will never amount to anything. If you've been called trash, I'm here to tell you God is in the business of recycling your trash and turning it into treasure.

I want to first thank my heavenly Father my Creator, Jesus Christ my Savior and the Holy Spirit my Comforter for leading me along this journey regarding my life.

I want to thank my wife and best friend Roseline 'Roz' Bennerman who is such a wonderful person and who has seen the good, the bad and the ugly through our relationship over the years. Thank you babe for not giving up on me and believing in the Vision and direction God is leading us in. Thank you for allowing God to use you so He can mold me into the person I am today; love you always.

Thank you mother (Mary B. Bennerman): I thank God for you loving me unconditionally and being so supportive. There's no words to say but thank you Mom, I love you very much.

Thank you dad (Ernest C. Bennerman) for dropping nuggets of wisdom during the latter part of your life on earth before you departed to be with the Lord. I Love You Dad, Rest in Peace, you will always be missed.

I want to thank my son (Terrell N. Bennerman) who turned out to be a very talented young man who's determined and purposed to impact this world. I love you son.

Thank you Apostle Mark T. Jones for being an example here on earth of how to be a Godly man who loves God and His people.

I want to thank each one of my sisters Andrea and Tameka for your laughter and encouragement; I love you ladies always, as well my brother Anthony. I'm praying that he will be all God called him to be.

Thank you grandmother Macy Bennerman for your wisdom and laughter. And I thank all my Uncles, Aunts, Cousins, Nieces and Nephews. I also thank my wife's family for being such an incredibly close family who welcomed me with open arms. I love each one of you and I want to say thank you for your support.

Thank you CFM family for teaching me how to serve and love unconditionally.

I thank my enemies for **Getting Me Fired UP** as I wrote this book. God allowed you to attack me so I will be stronger for those who don't have the endurance to fight back. I want to encourage my readers to have an unstoppable mindset and continue to speak these words to yourself over and over again...**NEVER GIVE UP; I'm not giving up**! Remember, you have greatness on the inside of you!

Contents

CHAPTER 1
Raised From The Dead

"The same power that raised Christ from the dead is inside of you."

Romans 8:11a (NLT)

CAN REMEMBER July of 1999, and how life has a way of bringing you to your knees and can leave you feeling hopeless with a trail of broken promises, broken dreams, unrealistic goals and unhealthy relationships. I can be honest with you because you are my friends and I believe you should be open and honest with your friends.

I was a broken young man who clearly lost his way and lost the fight in the dog. A puppy dog had a better chance of accomplishments then I did at this time in my life as I look back. I felt anything but "Fired UP" at that time; I felt "Fined UP". I had bills that were out of hand, along with broken dreams as I walked in my dysfunctional paradigm. Did you notice that I had to take responsibility for my own actions? I heard a wise person say, you have a right to be angry, you just don't have the right to take it out on me. I was the one who blamed everyone for my problems instead of looking in the mirror at me. I remember it like it was yesterday, as I sat in my recliner in July of 1999 on a hot summer morning recovering from a hangover from the night before, overworked and underpaid, sinking in quicksand, so quickly adapting to the mindset of someone who lacked motivation and purpose for his life. I decided to blame the "Man". See what I am talking about? Not taking full responsibilities for my life.

One of the greatest musical performers of all time, named Michael Jackson sang a song called "Man in the Mirror". I did not like the person I had decided to become until I heard a gospel preacher named John Hagee share the good news of Jesus Christ. He talked about Heaven, which I wanted to know more about, and hell, which I wanted to avoid any way possible. I fell to my knees and cried out to God... 'I need You,' and I realized Jesus Christ died for my sins. I'd broken his holy commandments no matter how much I tried to keep them. When I got up off the floor and wiped the tears from my eyes there was a peace that passed all understanding. Praise God...The God of the Universe!

Oh, what a wonderful message I heard that Sunday morning. I'm not being religious in any way; however, I'm just sharing with the world how my life was turned upside down. I ran to God, and He welcomed me with his loving arms, so I went out and purchased a bible. I was thirsty to hear more about how God had a purpose for my life and why I was here on planet earth. I wanted to forgive every person who wronged me and those I hurt along the way. The following week I went to a small Baptist church in Bethlehem, PA with about 60 members. They were very traditional, however I was able to be a student of the bible because I was hungry for change. Sometimes in life we want things so badly, we feel that we need it now without going through a process. I realized very quickly that who I hung around with was who I became. I would hang out with people like me or worse than me.

The moment I made a decision to change, things changed for me. I can remember several months after this new awakening that I had an opportunity to teach Sunday school class. Guess what? I flopped terribly! I was so embarrassed that the pastor was kind

> "You may be disappointed if you fail, but you are doomed if you don't try." Beverly Sills

enough to include me in his sermon. I wanted to find a rock to hide my head under and leave the church, if you know what I mean. If you want to be successful in life, you will fail miserably. You have to keep going, get back up and move forward. Here's a quote by Beverly Sills, "You may be disappointed if you fail, but you are doomed if you don't try." I decided that I've been running all my life from processes, so I decided to suck it up and allow God to do major work on the inside of me.

I was jealous of what others had. I wanted it by hook or crook. See, you have to remember when I was in high school, I wanted to be the coolest guy in school...Not! I wanted to impress all the young ladies who showed any interest....Not! I was teased and picked on by several people because I was not like them. I struggled to identify my talents and abilities because I was facing a war going on in my heart; I was looking for answers. Reaching out to the popular kids in school, saying to myself, *If only I could be like them*, I hated being me at that time in my life. You have to make sure you don't get desperate for anything or anyone; trust me, you will pay dearly for your lack of wisdom. This story reminded me of "Rudolph the Red Nose Reindeer"; they decided not to have him join in any reindeer games. Sounds funny, right? Believe me, someone who is reading this book can relate to what I'm talking about. Maybe you tried to fit in at work to impress your boss, or maybe tried to impress your ex girlfriend or boyfriend. Maybe you grew up in a house that was accustomed to manipulating your way to the top. I can remember working a summer job and received my first paycheck as a freshman in high school. I went out and purchased a designer shirt which was a knock off, with confused horses going upside down instead of right side up...I was trying to keep up with everyone else in the 80's. I thought I was the talk of the town; I went to school and guess what? I was the talk of the town in a bad way.

Let me ask you a question: are you out of the loop when you relate to people? How about your family, or maybe finances? Will you be honest with yourself and say, "I don't need people in my life to challenge me? Wrong. People are not your problem, you are the problem, and you need to deal with your dysfunctional habits. Most of us are on a mission to prove others wrong; however, I failed to deal with my own insecurities, which caused my relationship to be fragile. Imagine you are involved in a toxic relationship, and let's rewind to the point where you met this person for the first time. Ask yourself, is this person right for me? What are my standards regarding my life? Let's talk about some of your bad relationships and people who tried to give you sound advice, but you failed to listen and you were treated like trash. You deserve better than that! Who's abusing you?

Dave, why are you writing this book.....because I believe we must "Get Fired Up" about our purpose in life. You're not a mistake, no one has your fingerprints, your walk, your talk, nobody can sing like you. Remember, nobody can play ball like you, swim like you, write like you or have your creative ability. Stop being a copycat, and be YOURSELF! God loves you and He makes no mistakes. God gave me a vision for bringing change to all people in this world. He told me not to be afraid, He said I will face many disappointments and be hated for

> Stop being a copycat, and be YOURSELF!

His name's sake, however, He loves me greatly. He showed me people from all over the world being touched in a special way. Guess what, that vision is coming to pass as I travel around the globe to some fantastic places, meeting some incredible people. I want you to know, you are not a mistake. Don't you want to achieve your goals and live your dreams? **GET FIRED UP!** Unfortunately, most people work harder on their job than they do on themselves. I want you to Ignite Your Vision "NOW"!! When purpose is unknown, abuse is inevitable.

Let me pause for a moment and ask you this question: what's your purpose in life? Take some time and ponder this question, then write it down in your notebook or journal. I have come across people who ask, "Why am I here?" "What am I supposed to do?" Knowing your purpose gives meaning to your life.

I want you to picture a house that you're looking to build from the ground up. First, it's important that you're holding the correct blueprint and have the right tools, so you can start the right project. See, you have to start with the right foundation in mind. You must see the building before it's even built. People are not your project; you are your project. You cannot help build someone else up until you do the necessary work on yourself first. I know people, especially around the holidays, love to go shopping for family or friends, but fail to put any thought into the item they want to buy. When you give a gift to someone, make sure you put some thought into it, so that special someone will know you truly took time to show your gratitude. The bible says in Luke 14:28 (ESV), "For which of you, desiring to build a tower, does not first sit down and count the cost, whether he has enough to complete it?" When you're feeding your mind healthy things you can determine your outcome, which will bring you the right mental approach to lasting relationships for years to come.

Questions to Ponder

1. Do you take responsibility for your life?

2. Do you remember any embarrassing moments in your life within the last 5 years? Do you still feel embarrassed, or can you laugh at the event and know you've learned something?

3. Do you work harder on your job than you do on yourself? Or are you doing the things that will get you Fired Up about Your Vision?

4. What type of people should you have in your life to help you reach your goals and dreams?

5. What is your life's Purpose?

CHAPTER 2
Agent Of Change

"Life is like riding a bicycle. To keep your balance, you must keep moving."

Albert Einstein

F YOU WANT TO BE SUCCESSFUL, you must determine what's right and what's wrong. You must understand where absolute truth comes from; you need to bring everlasting change to your life, as well as to others you are supposed to touch. See, when you turn on the news channel you hear about the muggings, rapes, looting, wars and fraud going on in our world. Instead of speaking woe is me, say "Hey, I will decide to become an AGENT OF CHANGE." You need to ask this question: have I mismanaged my influence with people who cross my path? How about my family?

The time is now; we need to "Get Fired Up" and take action. When the storm of life comes, all of your efforts focused on the wrong stuff will mean nothing. There

> You must have a good foundation so you can withstand the torrential rains and winds of life.

might be someone who thought, if it looks good it must be good, but don't buy into this lie. There's a story in the bible, Matthew 7:24, where there were two houses: one was built on sand and the other built on a rock. The storm of life is going to come whether you like it or not. You must have a good foundation so you can withstand the torrential rains and winds of life.

Hollywood actor Arnold Schwarzenegger had a quote, "YOU CANNOT CLIMB THE LADDER OF SUCCESS WITH YOUR HANDS IN YOUR POCKET." I like that; we want something but we don't want to put any effort into being a good husband or wife or maybe a good employee or supervisor. What's the point of climbing the corporate ladder, and then you notice your home is falling apart, you walk in the door and your spouse tells you they want a divorce? Make sure your ladder is leaning on the right wall.

Let me share with you what happened to me back in 1993. I worked for a security company with a local trucking company, the next event changed my life. My house was about 20 minutes away, and, driving down a major interstate, suddenly, my eyes were very tired and I fell asleep behind the wheel. I had the craziest dream; I had such peace, and time seemed to stop. An automobile drove up on the driver's side blowing his horn, yelling at me to wake up as I was about to run into a concrete divider. I woke up, heart beating like crazy. I quickly pulled over, scared to death, like "what just happened here Dave?" My life flashed before my eyes and I said to myself, "God, thank you for sending me an angel to protect me." Oh my God, I should have been dead. What about you? How many times do you need a wake up call to get your finances in order? Are you running into a concrete wall regarding your marriage? Why do you refuse to seek wise advice regarding your marriage, yet you keep taking bad advice from someone who is not married?

Time to Get Fired UP! Don't you know you were created to solve problems and bring change to this world? Marriages are on the brink of death and you have the answer to a healthy marriage. Life is too short, so cherish every moment with purpose, achieving your goals and dreams so you can help someone else meet their goals and dreams. Whatever you need to do, don't waste time; last time I checked... God is not making anymore 'Time'. Your time will run out soon, some day all of us will die, so be deliberate about how to use your gifts and talents to impact this world. Please don't FALL ASLEEP on your Purpose; you have potential, and almighty God wants you to be the heaven this world is hungry for, but they will never know it if you keep it to yourself. If you're going to die, make sure you die on empty. You have an enemy that hates you and he's trying

> Almighty God wants you to be the heaven this world is hungry for, but they will never know it if you keep it to yourself.

to rock you to sleep with being average. See, you were called to greatness, and you need to get going.

I think about another pivotal moment in my life where I was traveling to Detroit, Michigan on a business trip with three other peers; we drove for hours, very tired, but we were close to our destination. Suddenly my eyes were closed for a few minutes of sleep; the driver at the time seemed alert, so I had no need to be concerned, as the driver was very talkative. Guess what? He stopped talking. I heard heavy rain hitting the windshield of the car, and I believe an Angel nudged me then. I woke up and noticed the driver was sound asleep, so I screamed out loud at him to "WAKE UP!!!!" I glanced over my right shoulder and noticed that on the passenger side a huge tractor trailer was barreling towards the passenger door where I was sitting. All I could see was this huge tire a foot away from my window, about to crush the vehicle... I thought to myself, "HELP ME GOD!" Miraculously we were not injured. "Thank You God I'm Still Alive" to be all You called me to be.

If you're going to make a major impact in this world, you have to "STAY ALERT" at all times, and you need to know, who am I riding with? Is it your family? How about your wife? Husband? Mother? Father? Friends? No matter the road you're traveling, it may call for a select few. Each person must be held accountable for what that individual does in their day-to-day life. Do you have someone who holds you accountable? You might be saying I don't do people; last time I checked, the cross that Jesus Christ died on runs up vertically, which signifies to "Love God", and horizontally, which relates to "Love people". I want you to think about all the great basketball players in the world. One person that comes to mind is Michael Jordan who had an inborn drive to win championships for the city of Chicago. Many people believe he's the greatest player of all time, however, he can't win ball games by himself, because it takes a team. Great players love to compete; they're usually the first ones on the court and the last ones to leave the court to improve their game. A sports reporter asked Michael Jordan this question: who do you want to play against? He said, Me! Stop trying to be better than so and so. Be the best YOU, enough said!

The real battle is going on inside of you. Two of the greatest days of my life were the day I was born and the day when I found out why...Powerful! Live life to the fullest and beware of your surroundings. You have to pay attention when you're on the road to greatness. Don't depend on any-one to stay awake for you; you need to stay focused on your assign-ment. You have

> Two of the greatest days of my life were the day I was born and the day when I found out why... Powerful!

to do this yourself. Now, you can have a great team of mentors who are in your corner constantly challenging you to keep pushing. You still need to divorce yourself from taking all the credit when things work well for you and none of the blame when things go bad for you. "Man Up" and take full responsibility as you drive on the road of maturity. Tons of opportunities will chase you, be-cause you can be trusted. Remember, you want to be a person of character and integrity. I happened to be surfing the computer one day and ran across a home im-provement show; several builders were out fixing run-down properties, and I noticed this young real estate in-vestor addressing a large mass of mold inside the bath-room walls, which is a big deal when renovating a prop-erty. Sometimes you need to call an expert to check your "walls" for mold. Do you have the right person in your life, who you trust to give you a honest evaluation of your progress? Do you get upset when they notice you have mold on your "walls"? When a person comes into your life, your life should be better, not worse. See, you have to check your personal property, "YOURSELF"...your HEALTH and EMOTIONS. You must identify toxic rela-tionships in your life that are causing your environment to be sick. You might be in a financial mess; don't run away from it, you must deal with it. Do you realize that you are an Overcomer? It's not over until God says it's over. You have greatness on the inside of you; if you see a problem with your family, job, or your neighborhood, re-member, you are the SOLUTION to the PROBLEM! We have to be proactive and not reactive when it comes to change. Stop looking for external things to hurt you. What can hurt you is the drama you face on the inside each and every day. For every cause there is an effect. You can have a beautiful garden, but if you don't take time to do the mainte-nance in your own yard, you will have major prob-lems. If you are a born again believer, you have

> For every cause there is an effect.

the power on the inside; you just have to flip the switch.

Here's a story in the bible: in John 5:7, where Jesus asked a man who was crippled, did he want to get well? The crippled man cried out to Jesus that he had no man to put him in the pool, so he can be healed. This man was in this condition for 38 years, Jesus said, do you want to be made whole? He never said anything about the lame man depending on others to help him into the pool to be healed, he wanted him to Get Fired UP, Pick Up that Stinky Mat that he was sitting on and get on with his purpose. Share your story with others so they can have hope for their lives; remember, we're talking about having a good foundation. I see many people crack under pressure and resort to alcohol and drug abuse. Life and Death are in the power of your tongue. Begin to speak life to your dead situation and let God do the rest.

All we can do is our best, so Get Fired Up about your life, refuse to remain mediocre and stop running from meeting to meeting to GET Fired Up. Getting Fired Up is on the inside of you.. Life will be your greatest teacher if you can endure the process. When you determine the course of your life, be clear about your objective, and be selective with who you get into business or personal relationships with. One thing about relationships is they need to be cultivated over time. It takes time to develop healthy relationships. My wife and I both made sacrifices, which did not happen overnight. We continue to study one another, living a life of selflessness. For example, in marriage you have to be on the same page if you're going to have a successful marriage. We must acknowledge to each other that we're different, and it's O.K. We must make wise decisions together and take some risks. No

Blame Game! Do your due diligence when you pursue any type of relationship or business opportunity. Your present thoughts determine your future.

Every now and then something happens in your life that turns a light on, and you begin to see things and people from a different perspective. Let go of unproductive behavior and attitudes that delay your promise land. Let's pick up the mirror and examine our flaws and admit that we have a distorted mindset on how we see things hidden deep in our hearts, since our childhood. The bible says in Philippians 2:5(KJV), "Let this mind be in you, which was also in Christ Jesus." See, it's very important to have a victorious mindset and not a victim mentality. I thought about Samson in the bible; I love these stories. God used

> Very important to have a victorious mindset and not a victim mentality.

ordinary people to do extraordinary things. Samson was a Judge for the children of Israel. He had a gift; he was very strong and courageous, however he lacked maturity and had an appetite for strange women. His parents wanted him to marry a nice woman who believed in the one true God. He refused to listen to wise counsel from his parents, due to pride. My question to you is, "Why haven't you started that business years ago?" Remember, if you sow good seeds you will reap a good harvest, but if you sow bad seeds you will reap a bad harvest. Samson was not willing to put a mirror to his face and say to himself …you fool! He needed to do something with his stubbornness, stop saying that it's everyone else's fault and take ownership for your life.

Why don't I like people, or why do people run away from me? Why don't I want to go back to school and get my High School Diploma, GED, or College Degree? Start that business? Why do I get passed up for promotion or why do I consume more than I produce? You have to look in the mirror and answer your own questions. Why is it so hard to commit to a relationship, why do I like to gamble, do drugs, drink, party all the time, spend the rent money on Friday and be broke on Monday? Enough is enough. Are you hearing what is going on right now? You have to break this destructive behavior, because you're sinking like the Titanic. God will place somebody in your life to throw you a life saver. Nevertheless, most people refuse to grab it. You need to stop running from the mirror and allow the mirror to show you what you look like. I remember a song that goes like this: "You better check yourself before you wreck yourself." When your engine light flashes on your dash board, don't keep driving; have a mechanic check the problem out.

Hopefully this book will help you grow and be all that God called you to be. You must surround yourself with positive people who encourage each other. Church is a good place to surround yourself with like-minded people. Once you take out the trash from your old mindset, you have to replace it with new ideas. You will start to see things from a new perspective. You need to set some short term and long term goals and look at them every day, then take action to remind yourself that this is what you said you will do. Let your goals be your teacher and follow through. Honor your word; hold yourself and others accountable for what they're going to do. If you're going to be successful in your particular area of service, you may need a mentor to cut your learning curve tremendously. I want you to make a decision that you are stepping outside your comfort zone; yield your gifts and talents that will bring change to the world. Whatever you do, please don't shy away from it, but confront it.

The bible says in Proverbs 22:3(NLT), "A prudent man foresees the difficulties ahead and prepares for them. The simpleton goes blindly on and suffers the consequences." If you want to be successful and do great

> Proverbs 22:3(NLT), A prudent man foresees the difficulties ahead and prepare for them. The simpleton goes blindly on and suffers the consequences.

things in this world, you have to prepare your mind and emotions and press on. If you step out and take a risk and it fails, that doesn't make you a failure. Only when you quit, learn from the situation and never give up. You have to learn to get back up. Failure will follow you all the days of your life until you delete the old information and replace it with new information that will change your world. Most people are terrified to try something different, in most cases because of fear (False Evidence Appearing Real). If you think and believe you will always be broke, you will be broke. You must believe you're blessed and prosperous. Remember that when life kicks you in the face and knock you down, if you can look up, you can get up. "GET FIRED UP" about the people in your circle. Get a pen 'NOW' and write down everyone who you would want in your inner circle so you can have a successful team that will support your dreams and outcomes.

There's a story in the bible in Genesis 37 about a young man named Joseph who had a vision for his life; he shared his dream with his brothers and, later suffered all kinds of difficulties. His brothers wanted him dead, he was sold into slavery, led away to Egypt, accused of rape and later thrown in prison. He could have said the heck with all of you. He could've thought to himself, I have every right to be bitter, however he made a choice to do the right thing. God gave him favor everywhere he went, being a blessing to other people while he was living in slavery.

I want you to think about the noise that's going on in your life. Did you have a dream you were excited about and told the wrong people? Did they become jealous and hate you for it? Make sure you wear the proper gear when traveling on the road to your destination. You will encounter strangers who will distract you from being successful; remember they tried to stop Joseph, and he loved them in spite of his painful past. How about you, have you tried to forgive someone who hurt you in spite of your painful past? Learn the same thing from other successful people: keep going and do not give up. When you run across people with no vision for their lives, don't hate them; love them and pray that they will understand the assignment God has for their lives.

The bible says, "Where there is no vision the people perish," (Proverbs 29:18a KJV). Jesus interceded for the religious leaders and the Roman soldiers and they continued to mock and curse him. "Jesus said, Father, forgive them for they do not know what they're doing" (Luke 23:34a NLT). You have to do the same thing if you want success in your life. Joseph was the son of a very wealthy man named Jacob who loved his son more than the rest of his sons. If you're raising children, strive to love each without favoritism; love them unconditionally. The last thing you want to do is invite jealously or strife onto your doorstep. How about your spouse? Do you put your favorite sports or TV show ahead of your mate? GET FIRED UP regarding your relationship; remember, stay focused and speak life to your mate and be an asset, not a liability. We see the family unit deteriorating because of strife and jealousy and these things weaken the union between the husband and wife. "Father, Forgive Us, for We Do Not Know What We Are Doing."

This book is to "Ignite your Vision Now." How many times do you need to get married, then later you're paying a visit to divorce court because you failed to work on your own personal development? You must get a clear revelation of why you are here. If you're doing drugs, and you keep saying one of these days I'm going to break this habit... Ok, let's talk about that for a moment. You said you're going to break this habit when you get ready. No, you have to replace your bad habit with good habits and you have to make a choice 'Now' to quit and get help. You can try to break them all day long, but you will always fall short because you failed to deal with the root of the problem. 'No More'; you need to be specific. I challenge you to make no more excuses. Make a decision and be deliberate about your life. Do you realize you have people who need to meet you in this lifetime?

Do you remember what we talked about earlier, that no one has your fingerprint, so why would anyone be so hateful? The reason is they lack vision for their life. Remember the bible scripture mentioned earlier, Proverbs 29:18a(KJV), "Where there is no vision, the people perish." You must Get Fired Up about who is in your circle, the people who embrace your dream. Be fruitful when you engage people of all circumstances. Get Fired Up about having good relationships, make a decision that you will be more valuable to those you meet at the grocery store.

Questions to Ponder

1. How have you managed your influence on your job or place of business?

2. How important is it to you to seek wise counsel regarding your relationships?

3. How important is it to you to have accountability in your life?

4. What does the word 'wholeness' mean to you?

5. Have you ever had a dream you were excited about and you told the wrong person? How did that make you feel? What did you learn from this? How will you share your dreams with others in the future?

CHAPTER 3

Pit To The Palace

"A mistake repeated more than once is a decision."

Paulo Coelho

ASK THIS QUESTION before we move on: who are you talking to and sharing your most intimate secrets and dreams with? Think about our friend Joseph, who I wrote about earlier. His brothers waited for the right opportunity to kill him. Are you trying to tell me that things have gotten that bad, and I now want to kill you? Maybe someone did you wrong by putting your business on 'front street'. Who do you blame? Start with yourself, because you should have seen or witnessed maturity in how they engaged with others before you shared your dreams with them. They threw Joseph in the pit to die. You might be in a pit in your finances, even though you're doing all you can to keep your business running. Study the pit so you can encourage yourself and someone else. Joseph was sold to merchants and traveled to Egypt.

He could've quit and said, just kill me, but he had a dream that kept him pushing on. See, when you know that you know no devil in hell can keep you from what God has for you, remember Joseph was working for Potiphar, an Egyptian officer to the Pharaoh. The bible says in Genesis 39:2(KJV), "And the LORD was with Joseph, and he was a prosperous man; and he was in the house of his master the Egyptian." What? All that Joseph endured and he's called successful. Yes! You heard it! He was willing to go through the process.

Will you allow God to mold and shape you to be the person you were designed to be? Are you willing to seek Godly counsel for your marriage so God can find you successful? Are you willing to stay in school and give everything you possess so you can change the world? You might want to consider finding work that complements your skills and talents. Maybe you tried to buy a house, however your credit is very poor. Remember, poor is a mentality, being broke is a temporary condition. Don't run from your temporary problems; seek out solutions and outcomes, which will break bad cycles and replace them with good ones that will get others following in the same direction. Let's continue with this wonderful story. Joseph's work ethic allowed Potiphar to prosper, not just moneywise, but with peace of mind. Have you ever had someone call you on the phone and you felt worse after you hung up the phone with them? Divorce yourself from blood suckers who will try to suck the life from you. Things may be going well, however you are restricted

> Poor is a mentality, being broke is a temporary condition.

from really experiencing life on your terms. You work for a company that pays you very well, however, you still feel like you're in Egypt (World System) rather than God's system.

The bible says in Matthew 6:33(KJV), "But seek ye first the Kingdom of God, and his righteousness; and all these things shall be added unto you." Joseph did not look out just for his own interest, but he made a decision to shine before God and man so the world's system would notice a difference in him, because he belonged to a heavenly kingdom system. Let me ask you a question: do people notice a difference in you? How about in your marriage, job or finances? I want you to hold on to your hat... Joseph was considered a pretty boy, and he smelled good; he used to wear gators, the finest suits, a 'COAT OF MANY COLORS'. Joseph had the best of the best. Now you have Potiphar's wife who wants to have sex with him while her husband is away. She represents a fallen system, as she made a decision to look attractive; she wore the finest dresses of Egypt. She was ready for a little fun, while the cat's away the mice will play. Joseph said, No!!

Are you trying to quit smoking, drinking or partying? You have to run away from toxic people; they want you to join them in there destructive lifestyle. The bible says in Proverbs 5:3(KJV), "For the lips of a strange woman drop as an honeycomb, and her mouth is smoother than oil." You need to focus on your purpose for your life, and watch out for dream killers; they love to come along and take from you, even after you said NO! This chick would not quit until Joseph gave in. You're probably wondering how come Joseph just didn't give in; nobody needs to know what's going on; WRONG! God knows. Joseph was a man of integrity and honesty who represented the kingdom of God, and his master trusted him to watch over his house while he was gone. Has anyone given you the keys to the store or office to lock up? Thousands or maybe millions of dollars in merchandise, but you did not allow temptation to destroy the trust that your boss, wife, husband, or relatives have in you. Joseph said, NO! He was accused of raping this woman, but she lied; he refused to give in to her demands, so he was thrown into prison. Joseph the dreamer did not see this coming from a mile away.

You pour your life into working on a project that will set you up for years to come with a great retirement plan, then you get called into the office and they ask you to clean out your desk because someone accused you of cheating the company out of huge sums of money. You feel betrayed. Joseph felt the same way, but here is something so powerful: God gave him favor, even in prison. He made a decision to encourage all, sharing how God is able to make all things new. He's the type of person you want in your corner when all hell is breaking loose. He could've said poor me, I never get any love. Everywhere I go, I always have bad luck, and my brothers sold me out, but NO! He was determined to be in Faith, Hope and Love.

These words are so powerful. Say to yourself; I will die in Faith, Hope and Love. Look at all the things life will throw at you. You're going to the school of life, and if you don't quit, you will get rewarded mightily. Does your private life match your public life? If you said no, you can change right now by doing the opposite of bad. I want you to take a few minutes and repeat this to yourself...I will die in Faith, Hope and Love. You believe in your dreams, but you failed to have goals so you can reach your dreams. All you have is a dream and you will be highly disappointed without purpose. Joseph had a dream about his brothers bowing down to him. He did not know he was training to be someone great. You're going to have many

> You cannot afford to be average.

more failures in life, so look at life as a lesson and learn how to respond when life throws you a monkey wrench. You will experience plenty of pain as you grow in your field of expertise. You cannot afford to be average. Get Fired UP about your life! You have to be hungry if you want to achieve your dreams and fulfill your purpose. Nobody is going to give you something for nothing; if you want it, you have to go get it, *Period.*

I hope you're learning something as we touch on real life stories that you can apply to any area of your life. If you want to advance, do a great job meeting needs; be the very best so the right people will notice you.

We now have two men who got themselves in some hot water and were thrown in prison; Joseph was assigned to look after them while they were in prison. Joseph noticed that the cupbearer and the baker looked troubled. Do you know of anyone who trusted you with their care? Joseph had the opportunity to focus on someone else other than himself. Very important to put away all distractions in your life so you can effectively counsel someone to make the right choices to improve their quality of life. You're not a mistake. Maybe you found out your daughter is pregnant. You did the best you can, but what do you say to your little girl who's too young to take care of a child? Or maybe your son told you that he's going to be a father.

You have to be clear and ready to open your mouth and address these issues. You went to the doctor for a check up, and the doctor pulls you to the side and says you have cancer, AIDS, a deadly disease; you want to know all the facts before you tackle the problem. I've learned earlier in the story that Joseph found favor with the warden. He was a likeable guy and served more than what was required. The baker and the cupbearer were troubled when each one of them received a dream. He asks the most important question of all time; this question changed his life and the lives of others. He asked the men, "Why do you look so worried today?" How about you? Do you ask that question when

> Your situation will change for the better when you help someone else get better.

you're engaging people you're looking to influence? The world is waiting for you to ask this question. Your situation will change for the better when you help someone else get better. The cupbearer and the baker shared their dream with Joseph, but were clueless as to what it meant. When certain problems arise in your life, do you say to yourself, no one can help me, no one understands me? Your help might be staring you in the face but all you can see is distraction all around you. You can be going through a major storm, facing serious challenges and God can be putting the right person in your pathway. Adversity comes before prosperity; Cross comes before a Crown. You must go through the storm to get to the other side. Joseph did not say I can't help you, he said God interprets dreams. He gave credit where credit was due; God is the one who knows our dreams. He humbled himself and interpreted the dreams of each one of these men; one guy was restored and the other lost his life. Keep doing well regardless of who recognizes you or not. GET FIRED UP about your life and know you are special and you have a special assignment in the lives of people. Life can be your greatest teacher if you have the right philosophy. The cupbearer's position of influence was restored, and Joseph said to the cupbearer; please remember me, when things go well with you. I have some bad news for you; help may not come right away until you deal with some old wounds that have not been healed properly. The cupbearer forgot about Joseph. Do you know anybody who said, they have your back, and later you don't hear from them? You might have gone to the bank for that loan and they told you, your application looks good and it will be a matter of days, then you'll receive that loan, and later they inform you that the deal fell through. Life has a way of smoking out any issues you have going on, so you will not sabotage any key people or things in your life. Let time have its perfect work and you will be glad you did.

Joseph ends up waiting two more years before his name was brought up again. You can't bring a world mindset into a kingdom mindset; you have been equipped to take on all of the variables you need to handle. Stop being in a rush and take small steps of progress until you graduate, then maybe you will be ready for the larger ones. I can remember a dark time in my life. I was looking for a way out of the drama I brought on myself. When you see poverty all around you and desire to seek change, let it well up on the inside of you from mediocrity to prosperity to impact the world, What I discovered was, there's nothing on the outside that can bring destruction, but what's on the inside of me will. I was the real problem and I needed to see the world differently from what I had been experiencing. You're broken from the inside, which will reflect how you look on the outside. I heard Tony Robbins say, "you don't have a resource problem but resourcefulness problem." You have to create the right job, you have to create the right opportunity, and you have to be the one to bring change to your neighborhood. The real you wants to come out, but you must face setbacks that will propel you to your destiny.

My greatest breakthrough came from my greatest disappointments, believe it or not. I felt like a loser with a capital (L); I was so angry at myself and felt like a jerk. Then I asked myself, why me Lord? He said, why not you? We can be very selfish most of the time, but we must be honest with ourselves. Sometimes you can be at the right place at the right time. The CEO 'Pharaoh' had a disturbing dream, which caused him to toss and

> My greatest breakthroughs came from my greatest disappointments.

turn all night long. The next day he told his official, he had a dream that troubled him and he needed the wisest men in the land to interpret his dream. You all remember the cupbearer, who was released from jail and went back to his old job working for the Pharaoh in a very prominent position? This fellow remembered Joseph at that moment. When you add value to the lives of people and offer them the service of gratitude, by giving 100 percent, people will talk about how well you provided great service to them.

Listen, stop chasing money and learn to serve well, be passionate about doing your job, and the right people will seek you out. I would like to share a true story with you that happened to me while traveling to Russia with my senior pastor Dr. Mark T. Jones, who's the founder of Center for Manifestation Worldwide Inc. located in Tampa, Florida. We were traveling to Russia sitting in the New York airport waiting for our departing flight, when we both noticed a piece of equipment was on the floor where someone could easily come along and trip on it. Dr. Mark Jones said to the employee working near the ticket window, "Excuse me you have a piece of equipment on the floor, I would not want anyone to hurt themselves, you might want to pick it up off the floor so no one trips on it." Here is the million dollar answer he gave him: "IT'S NOT MY JOB." Did you hear what he said? "Its Not My Job,"

It's not my job!

wow! I stood there shaking my head saying dude, just pick it up off the floor and go ahead about your business. I love what my pastor had to say to me that changed my life forever.   He said Dave; do you know what may happen if someone trips, falls and hurts themselves? I said what's that? He said, they may get a lawyer and sue the airport, which will cause them to lose money, which may force the airport to cut back on jobs; the manager or supervisor will look at all the employees and notice this particular individual doing just enough not to get fired, he or she might have been written up several times, showing up late. The first to bring disharmony among his co-workers usually are the ones to get a pink slip. What you do does affect other people as well. Be the one to give more than what you receive.

The cupbearer overheard the conversation, he went the extra mile and decided to be the giver in this dilemma by opening up his mouth and saying, "Excuse me your Majesty, I know a man who interpreted my dream when you held me in jail on my screw up. Everything he said about my dream came to pass just like he said." The Pharaoh went and told his officials to get Joseph out of the pit to bring him to the palace; he was able to interpret the Pharaoh's dream and was appointed second in charge; he was able to save his family and all of Egypt from famine. I really enjoyed the story of Joseph. You can go to the bible and read the book of Genesis 37. Believe me, you will be inspired and it will bring hope to whatever problem you might be going through.   The wealth of knowledge of God has a place on the inside of you and can help save your family and other families in the world. I want you to "Get Fired Up" and start eating right, exercise regardless of if other people laugh at you, go back to school to get your high school diploma. You have an opportunity to make a difference in someone's life. Joseph was destined to be 2nd in command of Egypt, but he had to grow up and that took some time. Don't rush the process; it's vital to your destiny.

One day I went to my mechanic to check my brakes because they were squeaking pretty loud. I thought maybe, I might need some brake pads, but what they found out was the pads had some sand which caused the irritation, the squeaking. Who's irritating you? People, career, job, spouse, school, finances or maybe some type of sickness in your body? You must first do an assessment and find out the cause. I want to warn you, you may find something that you may not want to face; nevertheless you can do it. You want to check things out so you will not cause further damage. I love reading books, and it's very important to my 'Now'. I hear some people say, I don't have to read, and I say you cannot afford not to read. Don't you realize your mind needs to be fed on things that represent you in every area of your life? If you can't find a job, then find out what your work is. How about you create work for yourself and for others. Time to take the limits off, and go for what you were designed to do in this world. You were created to work. A job can only earn you a paycheck, but your work represents your skills and abilities, which were designed to make you a fortune so you can be a blessing to others. Stop thinking

> ...your mind needs to be fed on things that represent you in every area of your life.

only about your four and no more.

When you hear your brakes start squeaking, stop and get it checked out before you break down. We must master personal self-mastery before we can move on to mentoring others. If you want to go to the next level, you are going to have to take ownership for your life and not point the finger at someone else. You must 'Get Fired Up' about your life and be part of the solution, rather than the problem, in this fallen world. The time is now for that family member to come home or maybe you put in application after application and nothing seems to be happening; if you keep speaking negative words out of your mouth, you keep getting the results you keep repeating to yourself.

Questions to Ponder

1. Who do you share your intimate secrets with? What are some of that person's quality traits?

2. Are you willing to give 100% in your career, marriage, or with your fitness, even if no one acknowledges you?

3. What are your skills and talents? Are you working in a field that complements your skills and talents?

4. Are you a problem solver? When a problem arises, do you seek out solutions to the problem or do you just complain, get discouraged and wait for someone else to come up with a solution?

CHAPTER 4

Speak To The Mountain

"If you are unwilling to risk the unusual you will have to settle for the ordinary."

Jim Rohn

TIME TO TAKE THE GLOVES OFF and go for it; don't allow fear to stop you from exploring the world of opportunity. If you're looking for work, speak life to your application. Here is something I always have done to seek employment; I believe this will help you out as well... ("Thank you Lord for waking me up this morning, I plan on putting in several applications today, lead me to the place you would want me to be so I can use my influence to bring change in a positive way to my employer, may the company be blessed and prosper because I am there. Someone there needs me to speak a word of encouragement, let nothing stand in my way that will prevent me from getting work at this particular company. I believe you will provide the necessary resources for my family and meet the needs of others, In Jesus name, Amen!") You need to find "work"; what you were created to do. Your body language says it all; spend time on your-self, because nobody knows you better than yourself.

If you "Get Fired UP" about your life, you will experi-ence a mighty breakthrough, so don't let temporary dis-appointments get you down; you may be knocked down, but you're not knocked out. Get Fired Up and punch back and say to yourself, I am not a quitter. So what, they laugh when you put in that loan application with bad credit. 'So what', you know yourself better than what your credit score says; keep pushing on so you can share your story with the world. You can't give up,

> You can't give up, you're closer than you think. Allow the process to take place as you're developing your character.

you're closer than you think. Allow the process to take place, as you're developing your character. Your talent may get you there but your character will keep you there. Remember, you cannot conqueror what you don't con-front. Deal with it and let's get going. You need to meet very important people in your future; God will connect them to you because he has big plans for you. Any prob-lem you may have, you will turn it into a great opportu-nity for others to keep going.

I lost my Dad several years ago; he was hit by a car and died instantly before help could arrive on the scene. He did not die in vain: I now help other young kids who are lacking the love from their fathers and let them know how much they are loved. I decided to turn tragedy into triumph, to walk in integrity and be all that I was designed to be. If you want to do great things, you have to let go of every negative thing that ever happen to you and pursue your dreams. Open your mouth and speak to your destiny.

Here are a few keys that will help you as you press on toward your future.

Here are seven steps for personal success:

1) Define the specific goal you want to achieve

2) Chart a detailed course with established deadlines

3) Make sure you visualize yourself attaining that goal

4) Be informed

5) Create a climate of confidence in every circumstance

6) Help others become successful

7) Connect with God

1) Define the specific goal you want to achieve:

Did you know that life changes only when your daily priorities change? Let's say you want to get married to the man or woman of your dreams; you must have a good relationship with this person if you're thinking about spending the rest of your life with him or her, and you must work on your own personal development. This is the first step for personal success. You will discover your strengths and weaknesses. You will find out very quickly if you're mature enough to have good relationships. See when I first met my wife, we had to first take action by

> Stop sucking up to people and just give the best of yourself to your assignment.

having communication and being honest about ourselves. Guess what? Stop trying to please people who really can care less about you, be real when you start a business, be real when you engage in relationships, and be real when you serve on a particular ministry. Stop sucking up to people and just give the best of yourself to your assignment. If you want to play sports, be the greatest you can be; allow the process for maturity to take place.

Let me share with you very quickly about providing maintenance to my lawn. My front lawn had a lot of weeds when my wife and I purchased our home. One of the first things we needed to do was pull up the weeds by the root. For every cause, there is an effect. When two people love each other, they have to deal with everything that will hinder them from growing together as they discover what the other person likes or dislikes. Allow the process to take place in your life to avoid a collision. Be specific and go after your dreams as if your life depended on it; you know what, somebody's life does depend on you fulfilling your dreams.

2) Chart a detailed course with established

deadlines:

Write it down, be specific and have a deadline. When my wife and I bought our home, we had to save a certain amount of money by a certain time frame, so we had to establish deadlines. I remember when I was in high school, throughout the school years, I had to take mid term exams, so they could see if I met the requirements to go to the next grade. You have to have deadlines. Imagine that you're dating someone and they drink and smoke all the time, and you see the potential in this person, however this person is killing themselves slowly. A true friend will tell you that you need to stop drinking or smoking and get the help you need to be set free from this destructive habit. I'm giving you 3 to 6 months to get your act together or I'm walking away. You care about spending time with this person, so you give him or her a chance to make the necessary changes that will impact their life. How about your marriage? Are you taking your marriage for granted? Don't close the door, but allow yourself to have healthy relationships with other spouses who have strong relationships. Put your foot down and say enough is enough. We are getting out of debt, we will start eating healthy and maintaining a healthy lifestyle by going on walks, and working out. A person who is working out, eating healthier and giving themselves deadlines will lose the weight. I believe you get the point.

> Put your foot down and say enough is enough.

3) Make sure you visualize yourself attaining that goal:

You have to see it before it manifests itself. I can remember after years of being apart, my wife and I remarried, and I had a vision of us having a beautiful wedding and taking trips and traveling the world. When you can visualize things, your life will be exciting. See yourself out of debt, see yourself buying a house. You have to see yourself starting a business or going to college to get your degree. See yourself pastoring a church or becoming the leader God has called you to be. See yourself excelling to do great things on the earth. Cut out some photos of houses or exotic vacations; see yourself

> When you visualize things, your life will be exciting.

having great relationships with family, friends and co-workers. See yourself losing some weight by pulling out your old picture where you were the smaller size and pinning it on your bulletin board or refrigerator, or tape it to your mirror where you wash your face. You must see it and visualize achieving your goal.

4) Be Informed:

Stay plugged into whatever your goal might be. Keep that excitement going and hang around people that will en-

> Keep that excitement going and hang around people that will encourage you and hold you accountable.

courage you and hold you accountable. Make sure you keep that momentum going. Think like an eagle; fly high, and stay away from pigeons. Get Fired Up! Trailblazer.

5) Create:

We have opportunities all around us each and every day. However, we can get so distracted by life that we fail to create opportunities and new ideas that will bring change to our lives. I believe God is always talking, however, we fail to listen to solutions to the problems we face on daily basis. I can remember when I was 19 years old; I must have obtained 5 or 6 jobs in one year, carrying around this entitlement spirit. I felt that companies needed to hire me because I had served in the military; thank you God for allowing me to humble myself and for giving me a burning desire to be an entrepreneur.

6) Helping others become successful:

The greatest feeling in the world is helping others become successful in life. Look for opportunities to use your gifts and resources to help someone be all they can be. When I go through the drive thru to place an order, I try asking the person serving me their name, and you should see the smile on their face as if they're saying that somebody really cares for them. If you're going out to a restaurant, say hello to the waitress and politely ask their name. Find someone and pour into them. Two of your main goals in life should be to live full and die empty. Reach your goals and dreams, and help others become successful. God will meet your needs in a mighty way when you surrender your will to His will for your life.

7) Connect With God:

What makes you tick? How is your spiritual life? When you feel like giving up, you will have plenty of opportunities to throw in the towel. If you're going to have any success, you must seek God to find out your Purpose. It's a wonderful feeling to know God is in your corner because He sees you yielding your life to Him and impacting lives for the good. You can have all the fame, awards, and money in this world, however if you don't have God in your life, you have a wasted life. I'm not taking it back, you heard me, and you have an unfulfilled life without complete surrender to Him. Sooner or later your battery will run out; you want to connect with Him not only in this life, but fellowship with Him for all eternity.

This book is about being sick and tired of being sick and tired. *Get Fired Up*!! about what you want to do and just go do it. Will it be hard? Yes. Will you cry some times? Yes. Will you

> If you're going to cry, cry to keep going, don't cry to quit.
> ~Eric Thomas

feel like giving up? Yes. Here's what Eric Thomas, a motivational speaker, said during a visit to a local school in Detroit. He said to a classroom of middle school students, "If you're going to cry, cry to keep going, don't cry to quit." What a great quote; keep moving forward no matter what. If you believe God placed a desire in your heart that will bless your family and countless others, take it from Nike: 'Just Do It'. The cross you wear around your neck represents a love toward God and people.

I used to drive a beautiful 1976 Buick Regal in high school. All I wanted to do was drive all over town but I lacked common sense, not checking the oil, so eventually what happened was the engine light came on and later I experienced the engine blowing out twice. This happens when your body starts to shut down due to stress: you are about to have a major meltdown. I treated my car like trash, because I failed to recognize the sacrifice my mother made. Do you deserve a good man or woman if you keep doing dumb stuff without realizing that a sacrifice needs to be made? The bible says in Luke 16:10a (NLT), "If you are faithful in little things, you will be faithful in large ones." We need to slow down and observe the direction of our lives and realize the process is extremely valuable to being the best person we can be. You have to learn from your mistakes so you don't repeat those bad habits. We have to create opportunities that will make a difference in our lives and the lives of others.

When I was young, I'd been to a number of funerals of loved ones and friends who went on to the next life. Now that really messed me up because I did not understand why a person had to die. It makes sense now, you were created to make a difference in this life. While you're waiting for your miracle, be a miracle for someone else's life. You're still alive, so why not make a major impact in someone's life today? Don't wait for tomorrow, just do it today. Fear and laziness want to rule your life, but it's a choice; choose to say no way. I don't know about you, but that's fighting words. You cannot let fear walk all over you; the bible says in 2 Timothy 1:7 (KJV), "For God has not given us the spirit of fear, but of power, and of love and a sound mind." There is another enemy that loves to knock on your door, and his name is 'Comfort'. So many people have fallen for this imposter who pretends to be a good friend to hang out with. If you are going to do anything great for the kingdom of God, you have to divorce yourself from comfort. Comfort loves to drink your Kool Aid, watch your TV, take long showers, stay out all night, and pay no bills. Do you remember the exercise bike you wanted so bad, that you turned it into a laundry rack? If this is you, you have to kick comfort out and say enough is enough.

Another imposter you have to also watch out for, his name is 'Just Enough'. He shows up to work and will do just enough to not get fired, and he will do just enough to have a relationship, and will do just enough to keep it somewhat interesting. He hates growth, he hates resistance, he shies away from long term goals, and lacks vision. He loves to hang out with common people; he wants to experience common things with common people enjoying a common life. I want you to look at 'Just Enough'; find a mirror, and say Just Enough, you have to go right now. Right now you have to make a decision to

> If you are going to do anything great for the kingdom of God, you have to divorce yourself from comfort.

make new friends called 'Uncommon', 'Greatness', 'Fearless', 'Courageous', 'Faith', and 'Strong' and welcome them into your life. I hope you can see yourself as a mighty warrior; go seize the land. You have to want it, no more blame game.

I want you to achieve all your goals and pursue all your dreams because you were made for this. You are important! But how effectively are you living? Are you using your influence to positively impact the lives of others? I love watching movies that inspire me to keep going; remember, motivation comes from inside of you. You have enough to get going and be the change in someone's life. Movies like 'Rocky' are like rocket fuel to get you going. You may get the beating of your life but get back up and try again. There is somebody for you if you will try again, learn from experience and make sure you don't repeat the same mistakes twice. If you want to have the type of life you always envisioned you must have the 'Eye of the Tiger'. You have to press on even if you feel like you want to quit. Look, if you want to be a great doctor, lawyer or basketball player or a great speaker, remember you need to become a student and learn all you need to know in your field. You must put in the work needed to propel you to your destiny, step up to the plate and take a swing; you have a chance to get on base but if you quit, you have no

> You are important! But how effectively are you living? Are you using your influence to positively impact the lives of others?

chance to get on base. Do you realize if you strike out 7 out of 10 times you're batting 300, and the major leagues will pay you millions of dollars to your bank account, so what about the number of times in your life you have struck out? Many successful people failed terribly and felt like quitting, however someone on the inside would not let them stay down for long. If you never struck out, then you must be perfect all the time, so I doubt if you've never struck out. There's only one person I know who was perfect, and that was Jesus. If you don't agree you can stop reading this book, but thank you for taking the time to get this far. I hope for nothing but the best for you.

Now, for those who have struck out multiple times, I want to coach you. Let's watch some game films and see what mistakes you're making and make the needed adjustments. You have to change your approach on how you see things and make sure you make the necessary changes that will bring you success. If you need a coach, go to my blog **www.igniteyourvisionnow.com** and sign up for coaching and don't forget to grab my free e-book; make sure you keep learning, take action and are committed to progress. How bad do you want it? You need to ask this question, because as I said before, what will you give now for tomorrow? Successful people don't wait for tomorrow when they can do something today. When you put on your tie and suit and go to work your family depends on you and the

> ...what will you give now for tomorrow?

company you're working with, so you need to perform at a high level. When your company is successful, then you are successful as a person, because you're going to give your best wherever you go.

We talked about Joseph, earlier in the book, and he prospered wherever he went, so stop chasing things and give it your all; you'll be greatly rewarded. Remember no one can judge effort. Someone may be more talented then you; however, no one can judge effort. Actor Will Smith shared a situation where his Dad wanted him and his brother to build a wall; Will looked at the job and realized, this job is going to take forever and sacrifices will have to be made. He later built the wall. The project took him 1 year and six months to completely build the wall; he laid each brick one at a time. Did you hear that? Each brick was laid perfectly. You can complete your project also.

I think about Jackie Robinson, who was the first African American baseball player to play in the major leagues. He faced a lot of obstacles, such as discrimination; he could've thrown in the towel, but he thought about future ball players who were looking to come up after him, and he made a decision to a leave a legacy. He thought about the young kids who wore his jersey, and his wife's willingness to believe in him. He knew his 'Why'. I'm going to ask you again, what is your 'WHY'? Remember, nothing just happens; what you do in life does matter. You must put the work in to propel you into your destiny, so when you take a swing, do like Babe Ruth, the baseball hall of famer: he points the head of his bat to the fence, confident enough that one of those pitches will leave the stadium. Find someone who you want to spend the rest of your life with, get in the game and get on base; surprisingly enough, you will get around the bases of life, which will bring you success in life. The bible says in Proverbs 12:11 (TLB), "Hard work means prosperity, only a fool idles away his time." We must not shy away from hard work: do things the smart way. Most people get their job mixed up with their work. The God of the universe wants us to work, He wants to manifest our gifts which will emerge on the inside you. Put your gifts to work, and you will have a perfect combination. Praise God!

Questions to Ponder

1. Have you ever given up on something? How did it make you feel? Do you have regrets even now?

2. Think of one situation or event when you didn't think you would make it through, but you did. What kept you going? In one word describe how you felt after going through that situation.

3. On a scale from 1-5 (1 being the least; 5 being the greatest), how much emphasis do you put on yourself to please others even when doing those things that are not authentic to who you are? Do you feel a sense of peace?

4. Do you believe you have a greatness inside you?

CHAPTER 5

Create Opportunities

"It is better to be prepared for an opportunity and not have one than to have an opportunity and not be prepared."

Whitney M. Young

CAN REMEMBER going from one dead end job to the next and before you know it, I was bored. Please don't be in a place like this; trust me, you were created to work, which requires vision. I want to share with you a story about a very talented musician who played the piano at a night club. One night, a distinguished gentleman was sitting at the bar demanding that this piano player sing a song. The piano player said to the hostile man, he's only here to play the piano. Well the customer refused to hear this answer, so the manager of the club insisted that the piano player sing a song. He opened his mouth and sang beautifully; he left his audience mesmerized. This man's name was 'Nate King Cole'. He took a chance and released his gift and he will go down as one of the greatest musicians this nation has every seen.

Remember, you must put your gifts, talents and abilities to work. I fell into a dangerous place. You must stay fresh and fervent in pursuing your passion; discover your 'WHY'. You can not be content just working at the dead end job. I'm not knocking a good honest job, just remember, the goal is to get better, 'Advance' is your new middle name as you progress in life. If your name is Joe Smith, you should see your name as 'Joe Advance Smith'. You're going to change your world for the better, so you have to change the way you think of yourself. This is what a winner thinks about; when 'Ambition' is looking for a job to meet his daily needs, while he or she is pursuing their dreams they will become laser focused. Let's look at 'Ambition'. He or she looks forward to the opportunity to speak to the manager with complete confidence, he or she understands the team concept that will help the company grow and prosper, which will create jobs for others. Your chances will increase greatly at obtaining the job and performing at a high level because you answered all the right questions regarding growth. Here is a list of six keys to being an effective person for any organization.

> You must stay fresh and fervent in pursuing your passion; discover your 'WHY'.

1) You must be a person of your word (Integrity).

2) You must be a person of good character.

3) You must work well with others (Team player).

4) Add more value to the marketplace.

5) Understand the direction the company is going.

6) Advance and train others (Leadership).

Ok, (Ambition) got hired at McDonald's; you're over qualified, but you really need funds to meet your daily needs until you get back on your feet, so you're hired and quickly work on the assembly line. Be the best assembly line worker the company has ever seen. If you give and produce more than anyone else your employer will notice the difference. Several weeks or months later, they decided to give you a raise and promote you. Be the best person you can be, do not hold back, and remember, your supervisor is looking at how you handle problems. Your boss takes notice and offers you a shift manager position with a raise increase. See what I mean, do your very best and opportunities will seek you out. 'Ambition' is doing well; they decided to make 'Ambition' store manager. You can go all the way up the corporate ladder, making good money while making a difference in other people lives.

> If you give and produce more than anyone else your employer will notice the difference.

Nothing just happens; you should be growing each and every day for the rest of your life. When you wake up in the morning, stop complaining about how bad things are; let us make the best of our day. You cannot stay where you are; the bible says we grow from faith to faith. You are a diamond on the inside but you can't become complacent in what God called you to do. If you want to succeed, you have to trust God. This will give you the know-how to fix your problem. Remember, you don't have to go through life alone. The children of Israel were looking forward to going into the promised land the easy way without any difficulties, but they were sadly mistaken. You will have to put your shoes on, trust God, and find a way to be the best person you can possibly be so you can impact this world. Remember you are built for giving your all to what life has for you. You will spot haters when you begin to get elevated up to what you were designed to achieve; keep serving, keep smiling, keep advancing, keep loving, and keep believing and you will be glad you did.

The children of Israel kept complaining and they already had a back up plan once they crossed the Red Sea, thinking about all the things they received while they were in 'Slavery'. They failed to think about the fact that they were slaves in Egypt. Let me ask you a question: who said you can't do something, or reach your goals? God gave you a vision; he wants you to accomplish your goals, so why are you not moving ahead, taking the necessary steps needed to get you closer to your objectives? You will have some people who will try to discredit your character, and bring heartache and pain; get over it, get up, and get moving in the direction you need to go. Please, take it from personal experience; you must take off those heavy weights that will slow you down from what you are called to do. You have to GET FIRED UP about your life; you need get healed so you can help someone else get healed. You need to be stable not only for you, but also for somebody else's deliverance. You have to be successful and victorious in your lifetime; get moving to your promised land and take someone with you. You are valuable; if you have a 100 dollar bill, is it not valuable? The answer is, yes! If I rip it in half and crumble it up, is this bill valuable? Yes! If I tape it back up, is it still valuable? Yes!

When you feel like giving up, speak to yourself and get fired up about your life; you have work to do. Go start that business, go read all the books that are in alignment with your vision. If your doctor gave you a bad report, get a second opinion; find somebody with wisdom so you can keep your faith up. I want you to pray for those who come against you, and speak life even if you don't feel like it. The road to success will have haters who want you to fall flat on your face, but champions always get up. You might have had a failed business, Get Back Up! You might be in a failed marriage, Get Back Up...love again. I'm here so you can Get Fired UP about your life and stop crying about how life keeps screwing you over. If nobody celebrates you, you celebrate you. Look;

> The road to success will have haters who want you to fall flat on your face, but champions always get up.

you're loved, because you're here to walk in your assignment. Stop looking over your shoulder or behind your back and just be the smart you, the brilliant you, the lovable you. Stop apologizing for how you were created, your color, nationality and so on. Nobody has your finger print, so get on with your life and discover the real you. "The righteous person may fall seven times but he'll get back up," (Proverbs 24:16 NKJV).

When I was a small child I would watch old sitcoms such as 'I Dream of Jeannie' and 'Gilligan's Island'. I would get excited about watching these half hour sitcoms. You don't have to twinkle your nose like 'I Dream of Jeannie', just start repeating what God said about you so you can bring glory to God. Don't buy into the lie that you are alone on a desert island; God wants you to have more out of life rather than sitting around eating coconuts. You need to work, stay busy, so you can be a blessing to your family and others. Why do you want to hang out with coconuts doing nothing? The enemy wants you to have a coconut husband or wife for only convenience, and then when they burn the toast you're ready to find another spouse, looking for another coconut to make you feel better about your fantasy life. You're watching a sitcom that's not real; you have actors who have to portray a part. See, that's the reason you're always getting hurt: because you're in love with an actor, 'Hypocrite'. I use to play this role until I found out why I'm here. You need to Get Fired Up; God wants you to come out of your comfort zone and leave your coconut friends who continue to pull you down.

Get inspired to change the world you live in. Once you become mature and stable, no one can lure you away from your destiny. Have you looked outside your door, have you noticed this world is looking for hope? They're looking for a solution to their problems. In the 4th grade, I loved reading comic books; I had a serious collection of books such as Spiderman, Superman, Hulk, Batman and Iron man. Let's look at some of the characteristics regarding these superheroes and see if we can gather some information and get some major victories in our lives. I hope you're saying to yourself: you're amazing, you're incredible to be around, and you're a mighty person that loves life. You might be looking for some adventure that will propel you to take chances, so you can be a fearless person. Somebody right now is reading this book, looking for a sense of adventure so you and your loved ones will be able to get to a place in your life where you can experience fullness. You're excited when you live on purpose. Maybe you want to be a crusader in your life, so you can bring change to your community. Stop looking at only your needs, but look to the needs of others. Will you get Fired Up 'Batman', and do something about it? Come on 'Iron Man', stop getting offended when people talk about you, or lie about you; you're stronger than a few ugly words. You are stronger than you look; keep going, you're heading in the right direction as long as you keep your eyes on God.

When they crucified Jesus Christ on the cross, He said Father, forgive them for they do not know what they are doing. He did not get offended, so why are you? Most people live 70, 80 or maybe 90 years; let me ask you this question: will you waste time complaining, or are you ready to own up to your mistakes? Say to yourself, I messed up, now I am coming out of this emotional wasteland and headed to my promised land. This is your year, you're ready to face new challenges, new opportunities. You used to be depressed and lost your sense of direction, and misery was your companion, but no more; you refuse to be a victim. Instead, you're victorious. People who are afraid to move outside of the box will tell you, your idea won't work. Let me ask you again, what are you willing to do to be different? You have to 'Wow' your customers by putting in 100% of pure effort. You are ready to conquer the world you live in every day, when you're out in the market place.

How about when you receive a bad report regarding your child? Say you found out your child is in jail. The enemy has picked the wrong one to mess with; you now pray with such passion, you now read and teach with such clarity. The enemy has picked the wrong one. You lost a loved one to a serious illness; be ready to fight back by loving the unlovable. No more staying up all night walking the floor because you found out the company you're working for is laying off. You now take action, developing your skills, going back to school. This is the day that the Lord has made I will rejoice and be glad in it. You now feel like a free agent and can work anywhere you choose, because you know you have the greater one on the inside of you.

Now that you've tapped into what this book is all about, make a decision: 'Get Fired Up' and go for what is rightfully yours. The bible says in Proverbs 13:4 (NLT), "lazy people want much but get little, but those who work hard will prosper." You are a world changer who decided to be productive, active, alive, wise, strong and courageous. The only one to stop you is you; you cannot blame anyone else for your lack of effort, only you. You were wired to produce; you were made to be fruitful by growing each day. Some people are in love with their remote control, watching TV, or eating chips, but they refuse to grow. Imagine two individuals who are both very sick with the same symptoms. The first patient gets the report, loses all hope and he later shuts down. The second patient says to himself, I believe things are going to get better because I choose to share every ounce of love, joy and peace that passes all understanding. When sickness comes ringing your door bell, do what you normally do; you look through the peep hole to see who it is. Wrong house, devil. I refuse to sign for sickness and disease; just because sickness is ringing your door bell does not mean you have to answer it. We need to stop receiving things in our lives without challenging the source.

When Jesus cast out demons, he did not get into a long dialog with evil spirits, he just said: shut up and come out. Say what you want to see; most people are frightened if they are successful. I want you to realize, if you want something bad enough, you're going to pay a huge price, but it's worth it. A few years ago I was driving on the interstate; I had no coins to throw into coin basket stationed at the toll booth. I had no other way to pay, so I drove through hoping not to get a ticket. Well 1 to 2 weeks later I received a letter in the mail saying I needed to pay. If you're traveling on the road to success, you're going to pay the price, and you're worth it, so pay your dues so you can share your experience with others. Some people need to loosen up and laugh a little bit, stop taking things so seriously. I love to watch funny movies that don't have all the filthy language, shows like the Three Stooges, Marx brothers and Abbott and Costello. I love these precious treasures; the bible says in Proverbs 17:22a (NLT), "A cheerful heart is good medicine." The enemy wants you to do the opposite, so you will be useless to those you were called to reach. I recommend you purchase these videos, and possibly watch these when life comes knocking on your door and you start feeling kind of down; look at yourself and say, I am an overcomer, I have joy unspeakable and remaining balanced is the key to being an Agent of Change. You must be armed with the Prince of Peace and gather all the tools and resources you need to live a victorious life.

I will continue to repeat this matter over and over until this plays in your subconscious. Don't stop chasing your dreams, don't give up on your marriage, don't give up when you get a bad report from your doctor, don't give up on your education, don't give up on healthy living, don't give up on your business, don't give up on ministry or people. I hope you get the idea; you will look back on this event in your life and thank God you re-evaluated the situation and took action. Remember, encourage yourself so that you will fulfill your assignment on the earth. I don't want you to buy into the wrong plan, because if you don't live God's plan you will be working for someone else's plan. I want you to grab a pen and a

> If you're traveling on the road to success, you're going to pay the price, and you're worth it, so pay your dues so you can share your experience with others.

piece of paper and write down 5 reasons why you are here. The bible says in John 3:30 (KJV), "He must increase, but I must decrease," so let someone else be important, find out the needs of the people you come in contact with and plant seeds of greatness into their lives. Talk less about your accomplishments and more about somebody else's. Opportunities are all around us, but not every opportunity is for you.

I was watching a football game one Saturday afternoon and saw a commercial of a madman with a chainsaw chasing a bunch of teenagers through the woods. They had three scenarios to select from, 1) Run into a house; 2) Jump into a sports car with the engine running; or 3) Run into the barn with chainsaws hanging up all over the place. Guess what? They selected #3. They hid in a barn with chainsaws; we have to make sure we make wise decisions if we're going to impact the world we live in. Many people overthink the choices that need to be made because they want to play it safe. You failed to seek wisdom on how to have a healthy marriage. Maybe you used to take drugs; you never asked yourself, why do I need drugs and who can I learn from to show me the right way to get off drugs? You might have failed in business, but you learned how to make the needed adjustments to go on. Effort will keep you married; effort will keep you on the right path to success.

You can have all the talents in the world but if you don't develop your skills, you're cheating yourself. Your skills will not keep you in a place if you don't develop your character. You need to have several mentors in your life. A good accountability partner holds you to what you said you will do. The day you said, I don't need to grow up and be taught, you're done; you can stick a fork in it. Trouble will come knocking on your door looking for you the moment you refuse to embrace personal development for yourself. You have to Get Fired Up and stay hungry always, keep seeking and strive to be successful always. Life is so short; do not waste time, and don't ever say to yourself that you refuse to learn. You have to decide that you are going to be part of the 1% that will make a decision to impact many lives. Ray Lewis says, "Greatness is a lot of small things done well." He sowed seeds in my life and now it's my chance to sow seeds into your life. If you want to be successful in every area of your life, you have to do the little things others are not willing to do. God has given you gifts and talents, so turn disappointments into opportunities. Allow disappointments to be your greatest teacher.

> Your skills will not keep you in a place if you don't develop your character.

What are you willing to give to be great, to have a great business, great marriage, great finances, great relationships, great eating habits, great goals, great home, great kids, great community, to be of great service to those in need, to be a great pastor, or a great leader? You may come from a different background, or race, or you have some type of disability. I have good news for you, Google "Nick Vujicic". He goes all over the world inspiring people from all walks of life as a motivational speaker and evangelist. He was born with no legs and arms, however he refuses to feel sorry for himself. Yes, we may fall down but I refuse to stay down. People are going to say terrible things to bring you down, so you better talk to your spirit on the inside to motivate you; once you do great things, you will be a target. Everyone who does not like you will discourage you to try and knock you off your game; make sure you're the one that's standing, that's living.

It's very important that you see where you're going before you get there in the natural. Walk by faith, not by sight; you need to have faith. If you lose your job and the rent is due, you need to

> ...make sure you're the one that's standing, that's living.

have faith to believe God will give you insight to find another job that will bring out your skills and talents. Do me a favor: learn what you need to learn and be strong and courageous as you pursue your goals and dreams. Why is it so important for you to achieve your goals?

Give me 5 reasons why it's so important for you to achieve your goals.

_____

_____

_____

_____

_____

_____

_____

_____

_____

_____

_____

_____

_____

_____

_____

_____

Questions to Ponder

1. Do you have an accountability partner(s)?

2. Name one thing that you would love to have in your life that you don't currently have. Are you taking daily actions steps to acquire that one thing?

3. How do you stay invigorated and on fire to stay focused on your goals?

CHAPTER 6
Mission Of Love

"Love is The Only Force Capable of Transforming an Enemy to a Friend."

Dr. Martin Luther King, Jr.

ONE HOT SUMMER DAY in Florida, I met a young man who looked so defeated and out of touch with life. I walked up to him and said, why you are here? I mentioned that God put a gift on the inside of him and nobody can do what he can do. You should have seen the look on his face; he had such a glow, and he was ready to be an Agent of Change. See, you look at the opposition and notice you have a golden opportunity to do some amazing things in this life. If you are able to withstand disappointments, you will be able to be strong in your faith. This young man was surrounded by poverty, despair and hopelessness. I am here to tell you, that you are better than you think.

Do you have a dream that will impact this world?

Stop wasting time and go help somebody achieve their dreams. We have so many people chasing fast money; give it up and chase God. Stop hurting yourself and make a mission to love others; that is the key. Speak life to that person, to your neighborhood, to your family, to your finances; speak to that sickness that's trying to attack your body.

You need to have the right people in your life and remember, whoever cannot increase you, will eventually decrease you. I want you to observe who is speaking to you; look around at your friends and do an evaluation. If you care about your friends, you must get out of the pit first, and then you can help them out. I want to give you some principles that have helped me, and I'm sure they will help you. Happiness is forward movement doing the right thing. I've run

> ...whoever cannot increase you, will eventually decrease you.

across many individuals who fear taking chances; they're comfortable, living safe, don't want to advance, living paycheck to paycheck. Let me ask you a question; are you truly happy living average? Get Fired Up! And let's stir up the greatness within you. You bought into the lie that you are average. You are an expensive automobile; you were not created to sit in a garage. You were created to have movement and explore the possibilities. You are a trailblazer, not a follower. Remember, small steps equal progress. If you truly care about your family, friends, or the city you live in, make a decision and just do it; you know you were created for more. This book was created so you will get off your butt and seize the land. Come on 'Columbus', time to set sail and explore the new world. You can't have the relationship you always wanted if you don't take the first step to a lasting relationship. See, I want you to stop blaming others. Time to pull up your big boy or big girl pants, be mature adults and find a resolution to your current problem.

The bible says in Matthew 16:18 (NLT), "Now I say to you that you are Peter (which means rock), and upon this rock I will build my church, and all the powers of hell will not conquer it." Make sure you're made of the right substance, found only in God our Creator. If that's not possible, be graceful and move on with no hard feelings. If you decide to follow the blueprint to a victorious life, you can apply the same thing to your emotions, job, career or business.

I would like to share with you a bible story in 2 Chronicles 10, about a man named Rehoboam, who was King Solomon's son and was appointed king of Judah. As a newly appointed king, he now had to

> Make sure you're made of the right substance, found only in God our Creator.

make the hard decisions of how to rule his kingdom. The people approached the king to voice their dissatisfaction of how they were treated. So, King Rehoboam decided to first seek advice from the wise elders, they understood and had prior experience with the people. They suggested he be more favorable to his people. Rehoboam also sort advice from his peers, but they were not as knowledgeable about how to rule the people. They suggested he be even more strict then his father was to the people. Unfortunately, King Rehoboam decided to follow the bad advice of his peers which eventually caused disaster in his kingdom.

You must have a servant's heart in every area of your life if you want to live a purposeful life. Be a giver and not just a taker. King Rehoboam's kingdom was divided up and many people in his kingdom rebelled because they felt he was not hearing their concerns. You are a person of discernment, when you come in contact with a person of wisdom and knowledge that can help you get to your destination sooner. I love sitting down with an OLDER wise man and woman. I say again, close your mouth and listen, so you can cut your learning curve. You can come across a younger person full of wisdom and benefits as well. Whatever you do, make a wise decision in your marriage, in your family and your business ventures. We respect the doctor when they give us a report regarding our physical bodies; they're only sharing with you the facts based on the information from the lab work, however Jesus is my healer and He is absolute truth. The greatest feeling is living on purpose, so you need to find that 'Why'.

Here are six reasons why you need to write down your goals.

1) Goal setting is spiritual
2) Goals are statements of faith
3) Goals are the focal point of my energy

4) Goals keep you in steady pursuit

5) Goals bring forth rewards

6) Goals build your character

Here are two common mistakes when we set goals:

1) We love to set them too low

2) Too anxious for them to come to pass

Make sure your goals honor God, so you can change the world you live in and Get Fired Up for the next generations. Make sure you have fun and be deliberate about your goals, and always do the little things, and soon you will be equipped to handle the big things. I was doing some work on my computer, when I noticed a YouTube video. The title to the video was called "The World's Ugliest Woman." The video had several million views, so I was intrigued to see how this young lady looked. The person who put the video up failed to understand her disability that caused her to look this way; God used this incredible woman's story and showed the world He's able to help anyone overcome great odds and adversity. Lizzie Velasquez's story of pain, passion, love and courage will leave you inspired for years to come; see how relentless she was despite the ugly words people called her. She turned her pain into passion and now she travels around the world impacting lives, regardless of her disability. Have you been criticized for being too tall, too short, too black, or too white? Don't allow someone's ignorance keep you from reaching your goals and changing the world. If you're going to seize this opportunity to be a trailblazer in your family, remember you must get past what people think about you. Look at what God says in Isaiah 61:3 (KJV). "HE WILL GIVE YOU BEAUTY FOR ASHES." You have to see the glass half full instead of half empty, if you're going to be a world changer. Take the limits off and stop making excuses for why you can't do what God has called you to do. When you hold on to your history, you do it at the expense of your destiny. If you don't use your muscles, you will lose them. The same goes for your energy; see things from a different perspective.

According to the American Foundation, 100,000 people commit suicide each year due to hopelessness. You are the one to reach them with words of encouragement, words of hope, words of faith; you were made to be uncommon. This book is to inspire everyone who reads it to reach for the heavens. We want to reach our youth and beyond and decrease the number of suicides here in America and around the world. If you want to make a major impact, you need to take time and hear what's troubling the individual; look for signs and notify help right away. We have to be the light in this world by how we maximize our life to its

> According to the American Foundation, 100,000 people commit suicide each year due to hopelessness. You are the one to reach them with words of encouragement, words of hope, words of faith; you were made to be uncommon.

fullest; leave no unfulfilled dream undone, because someone's very life may depend on it.

Don't wait any longer; pursue God. He gave you a dream to be a nurse, go do it; you want to be the first to go to college, go do it. Nobody can stop you but you, so reach for the mountain and GET FIRED UP about your life, because you only get one chance in this lifetime as long as you're breathing. Proverbs 29:2 (NLT) says, "When the godly are in authority, the people rejoice. But when the wicked are in power, they groan.".

> Proverbs 29:2 (NLT) says, "When the godly are in authority, the people rejoice. But when the wicked are in power, they groan."

You were made to rule things, not people; you have the potential to help someone else discover their creativity. Get serious about your life; you were made for more than what you are producing.

I can remember, one morning the sky was very gloomy and I saw several sanitation trucks heading to the dump site to unload several tons of trash. You may know a person with gifts and talents being wasted; don't allow your God-given abilities to be thrown in the trash by bad mistakes, missed opportunities, failed relationships, broken promises, and broken dreams. Notice what you find in a dump: lots of garbage, rodents, and dead dreams; nothing produces at the dump. You have to be bold as a Lion if you want to pursue your goals and dreams; if you don't have that 'WOW' down in your heart to pursue what you are passionate about, you're just dreaming. Life happens and you will have your share of setbacks, maybe a divorce, or a death in the family. Reality sets in very quickly, and you can't afford to start reading a book when all HELL is coming at you. Build your house now with the right substance, which will last forever. You have a choice to choose the reality that will keep you moving in the right direction.

I can remember when I was 13 years old my friends and I would go downtown to see a karate movie. We would normally have to catch the bus, and one of the things I realized was, you will see many passengers get on and off the bus. If you're looking to get on, you have to pay the price; what price are you willing to pay that will take you to your destiny? When you're ready to get off you must take 'ACTION' you must make a 'CHOICE' to ring the buzzer so you can get off and reach your destination. Don't let anyone trick you into believing you have no choice. If you make no choice, you just made a choice.

You may know someone who's always in the 'dump' in their thinking and refuses to get off the bus; don't let life keep you in the dump, ring the buzzer and let the driver know you want to get off the bus. God will give you beauty for ashes, God will take your

> If you make no choice, you just made a choice.

trash and turn it into treasure, so stop feeling sorry for yourself, stop being in the dump, and GET FIRED UP and do something about it, to better your life and those around you. No one is exempt from bad things happening. You are aware that bad things happen to good people, and no one can escape from hardship and disappointments, however if you respond well, you will be developing character while you're going through your storm of life. The last thing you want to do is live life in the rearview mirror, but look ahead into your future; remember trash deteriorates at the landfill, flowers exuberate in the meadows.

Life and death is in the power of the tongue; you have to choose what you're going to eat so you can have a healthy lifestyle. If someone gives you two apples, one is rotten and the other is good, which one will you choose regarding your personal life? No one can make the choice for you, but *You*, feed your mind and network with people in your industry, or fellowship with like-minded people who will encourage and support you. Stop waiting for someone to constantly pump you up all the time; get in touch with your spirit man, and talk to God and ask him to give you the strength and boldness to overcome any obstacles or setbacks you will encounter on the road called life. You want to continue to motivate yourself on a daily basis if you want to achieve all that God has for you.

Questions to Ponder

1. Are you an asset or liability? Assets increase in value. Liabilities decrease in value.

2. Are you keeping your goals current?

3. Whose life are you impacting? Are you currently mentoring someone?

4. What are some of your greatest talents or skills? Ex. Are you a singer, do you love to bake, are you creative, etc.

CHAPTER 7
When You Die, Die On Empty

"The Greatest Tragedy in Life is Not Death But a Life without a Purpose."

Myles Munroe

WHEN I WAS A CHILD, I wanted to be the person everybody liked to be around, but you need to make sure it's for the right reasons. Be wise when you engage certain individuals in business deals; get to know them and see if they are a person of character and integrity, which will bring you unlimited resources for your business so you can have the success you love to have as you build your business. Dream killers have a passion for how bad things are and why you should not try that new business; look ahead to new opportunities. As long as you're breathing it's never too late to go back to school after you had a baby. Success intimidates most people so that they quit before they even take their first step. When you die, you do not want to have any regrets;

fulfill every goal you want that will bring God glory.

When you have relationships, make sure they're meaningful, and not superficial. I want you to know, this is your year to be about your Father's business; don't just talk about it, be about it. Building a life of significance and creating a legacy for generations to come, they both come with a heavy price tag. Real value means being willing to get your hands dirty. You have to have a well-cast vision for your life that can be commonly shared by all members of your team, family, friends, mentors, school teachers, coaches, pastors and leaders. "We must effectively communicate, we must realize that we are all different in the way we perceive the world and understand it as a guide to communication with others."—Anthony Robbins.

It's very important that while fear and anxiety will be talking to you very loudly to abort, you have to talk to yourself and say, I will not quit, I must keep going no matter how I feel. The acronym for fear is False Evidence Appearing Real. One thing about fear is its job is to paralyze you, but don't give it any thought; if you want to achieve your goals and dreams you must be stubborn about quitting on yourself or better yet, on God. I can remember in my own life, once I graduated high

> "We must effectively communicate, we must realize that we are all different in the way we perceive the world and understand it as a guide to communication with others."
> Anthony Robbins

school, I joined the Army; I later went to school and one of the things I had to face was leaving the state of New Jersey without having any family members around. See, I was experiencing a new world, things were moving so fast, and I was terrified of what I had to endure for several months. However, I was committed to learning something different that was necessary not only for my benefit, but for the lives of my fellow soldiers. If you want a successful life, take no shortcuts; be very deliberate and focus on the task at hand. I lost my way of thinking and took on the Army's way of thinking: a lean, mean, fighting machine. You have to see yourself, when you are chasing your dreams, so you can bring change to you and your family. The world is waiting for the manifestation of the sons of God. Yeah, don't waste a perfectly good life; you were created for more.

I remember a time when I was coaching one of my clients, and the enemy tried to cause distraction to get me to lose hope in this person. Focus on what you need to achieve for that particular day. "Distraction" loves to visit your home, workplace, and business place. You have to define what a distraction is to you. "Distraction" loves to harass people with "No Vision". I grew up in Newark, NJ, and every time I would go home to visit my family I would drive around my old neighborhood and notice "DISTRACTION" lifting up its ugly head. You will notice "DISTRACTION" loves to hang out in neighborhoods with no vision. The bible talks about the children of Israel being slaves in Egypt; God called Moses to lead his people to the promised land, however due to their lack of faith, the children of Israel wandered around in the wilderness for 40 years. They complained about what they didn't have and overlooked what they did have.

Let me share with you two different illustrations here. The first participant in this story is a young man called "JUST ENOUGH" who finished high school, then he got a job at a local restaurant. He started out as a cook, and he was content with his pay, so he stopped growing. He refused to get the needed training that would bring increase into his life; he refused to read books in the industry he was working for. Here you have "MORE THAN ENOUGH" who was in the same situation, however this person decided to GET FIRED UP! And be all God created him to be. He started out cleaning tables, always lending a helping hand, well-respected by his peers; he took great pride in his work because he understood growth, he invested in needed training in the area of leadership and management, and later he was promoted to store manager. He was pursuing his dream, bringing value to the restaurant, and now he's an owner. You might say, what happen to him? He had a vision for his life, he took action, and he refused to take handouts; he understood why it's so important to create jobs for his community. Each employee takes ownership in creating a culture.

The enemy doesn't know what to do with this information. Take the limits off, and start seeing yourself victorious. Everything you do, do it to the best of your abilities and watch out. Make

> Make sure God is involved in your decision making, put him first and He will do the rest.

sure God is involved in your decision making; put Him first and He will do the rest. The bible says in Matthew 6:33 (ESV), "Seek first the Kingdom of God and his righteous and all these things will be added to you." You don't need to run after fame and fortune, you need to seek God's will for your life. You cannot take your money with you when you die, so you might as well get the right perspective on money and why it's necessary for you to have it in your possession. Think of all the good you can do, the needs you can meet not just for you and your four but for others. The greatest feeling in the whole world is helping someone get from one place to another.

I cannot tell you enough how I made some unwise choices, some costly mistakes that cost me years of delay. The bible says in Proverbs 22:26-27 (NLT), "DON'T AGREE TO GUARANTEE ANOTHER PERSON'S DEBT OR PUT UP SECURITY FOR SOMEONE ELSE. IF YOU CAN'T PAY IT, EVEN YOUR BED WILL BE SNATCHED FROM UNDER YOU."

I can remember a time in my life when I had a 480 credit score, which says a lot about me? How about you? Do you have a '480' philosophy regarding your marriage? How about a '480' bank account; is it bad or good? When you look in the mirror, do you see '480'? Do you hang around '480' friends who are no better than you? You want to be around people who will challenge you to rise to the surface. These people are relentless, goal-oriented people; please understand they are not perfect people but excellent people to be around. They failed many times in life than they have had success, however they have a no-quit, no-nonsense attitude. You have to divorce yourself from a '480' mindset and take on an '800' mindset. How about you make a decision and have '800' relationships. The bible says in Philippians 2:5 (KJV), "Let this mind be in you that was also in Christ Jesus." You cannot stay poor in your mindset; you will not be able to help those individuals if you don't have a changed mind. Success is many things to different people; to me it's what you become while you're on your way to the final destination. A successful marriage is what you become on your way to maximizing both parties who are destined to be in this relationship.

I hope you have found great value in this book; remember as we close, the world needs your gifts and talents. Someone out there might be the next President, Prime Minister or maybe a scientist for a cure for cancer, aids or various illnesses that humanity will benefit from greatly. You'll be the one to bring change to this generation and to generations to come. When you die, die on empty; don't take all your gifts and talents to the grave. The time is now, so let's Get Fired Up and change our world. Thank you for taking the time to read this book; this is a **GET Fired UP** Revolution that will cross all barriers. May God Bless You in ways you cannot imagine.

Questions to Ponder

1. Are there relationships you need to reassess?

2. Are there areas of your life you need to re-evaluate?

3. Are you Fired Up about your Purpose in life?

ABOUT THE AUTHOR

Coach Dave captivates his audience from all walks of life, developing needed skills that will bring transformation to his listeners for generations to come through humor and visuals. He's well received and loved by his students (mentees) and colleagues. As a Certified Personal Life Coach for over 20 years, Dave focuses on transforming the lives of people through goal setting, life planning skills and accountability measures.

As your Personal Coach, together we can reach YOUR goals!

He grew up in Northern New Jersey surrounded by violence and poverty, with a loving sister and a mother who instilled hard work and perseverance into their lives. After finishing high school he joined the United States Army and later met his wife, Roseline 'Roz' during his college years, and they are blessed with one son, Terrell. Dave took a wrong turn in life and discovered problems, heartache and disappointment do not discriminate. He lost everything that was dear to him and made a decision to seek God for healing and restoration.

Now he empowers countless individuals in his surrounding community, and shares his faith and love for God with many individuals from diverse cultures. In 2012, he was ordained as an Evangelist and he travels around the world encouraging people to live on **PURPOSE**.

COACH DAVE BENNERMAN

CEO & Founder of Ignite Your Vision Now

Visit Coach Dave's Website at:

www.igniteyourvisionnow.com